THE CHURCH
Learning About GOD's People

For David and Kristen
and all my other Explorers
of the faith.

Concordia Publishing House, St. Louis, Missouri
Copyright © 1983 Concordia Publishing House
Manufactured in the United States of America

All rights reserved. No part of this publication may be reproduced, stored in a retrieval system, or transmitted, in any form or by any means, electronic, mechanical, photocopying, recording, or otherwise, without the prior written permission of Concordia Publishing House.

THE CHURCH

Learning About GOD's People

Written by Carole S. Matthews/Illustrated by Jim Richter

Trinity Ref. Church Library

Publishing House
St. Louis

What is the Church?

The Church is not a building
made of stone and brick.
Christ's Church cannot be found in a special place,
on a particular day, at a certain time.
The Church can be everywhere, anyplace, anytime,
for the Church is people—just like you!

The Church is full of children—large and small.
The Church is men and women—bankers, farmers,
merchants, and students, just to name a few.
The Church is mothers and fathers,
aunts and uncles, cousins too.

The Church includes people of many colors
—brown folks, red, black, white, and yellow.
People who live in every nation
and speak many different languages
are part of Christ's Church.
The Church is tall people, short people;
some thin and some who are fat.
Makes no difference what their size or shape,
they too can be a part of the Church.

The Church includes those who can run
and those who need a little help;
those who are able to see and hear,
and those who can't.

The Church is rich people who live in large houses, and poor people whose houses are not so grand. The Church is **all the people,** everywhere, anyplace, at any time, who believe that Jesus is their Savior.

We need the Savior, because we sin.
God wants us all to love and obey Him.
But often we don't obey.
Sometimes we don't even want to obey.
Still, God keeps on loving us.
Jesus showed how much God loves us.

Long ago God sent His Son Jesus to live on earth as a man.
Although Jesus was a man, He never disobeyed God.
He was perfect in every way.
Jesus willingly suffered and died on a cross,
but rose from the dead to live again,
so that we all might be forgiven our sins.
One day we will live with Him in heaven.

Before He went back to heaven, Jesus gathered His disciples around Him. He told them to go out into the world and help others to be disciples too. This is the way the Church began.
He promised that He would be with them always until the end of time. Then Jesus returned to heaven to be with His Father.

But, just as Jesus promised, He sent His Holy Spirit
to guide and lead the Church
Christ's Holy Spirit is still with us today.

The Holy Spirit lives in all those who believe in God the Father and in Jesus Christ the Son of God, the Savior of the World. Jesus uses people to continue to do His work here on earth.

That is why the Church is people
and these people are called the **Body of Christ**.
Our body has many parts;
so does the Body of Christ—the Church.
All the parts of our body have
something important to do.
So it is with the Body of Christ—the Church.

The people in the Church
are the parts of Christ's Body,
and each person has something different
but important to do.
Some are His hands to help others.
Some are His mouth to tell others of God's love.
They all work together to do Christ's work.

We come together to worship in a church building,
but this is not the **Church**.

Christ's Church is everybody, everywhere, anyplace, at any time,
who believes in Jesus; for Jesus taught us:
"Where two or three come together in my name,
there am I with them" (Matthew 18:20 NIV).